D1279952

Caffeine

Valerie DeBenedette

—The Drug Library—

Enslow Publishers, Inc.

44 Fadem Road   PO Box 38
Box 699   Aldershot
Springfield, NJ 07081   Hants GU12 6BP
USA   UK

To my parents, Rachel and Jerry DeBenedette,
and to Bernard Cullen

Library of Congress Cataloging-in-Publication Data

DeBenedette, Valerie.
      Caffeine / Valerie DeBenedette.
         p. cm. — (The Drug library)
      Includes bibliographical references and index.
      Summary: Examines the history, physical effects, and
social aspects of caffeine, the most commonly used drug in
the world.
    ISBN 0-89490-741-7
    1. Caffeine—Juvenile literature. [1. Caffeine.] I. Title.
II. Series.
QP801.C24D43 1996
615'.785—dc20
                            95-51807
                              CIP
                               AC

Printed in the United States of America

10 9 8 7 6 5 4 3

Photo Credits: Bernard Cullen, pp. 7, 55, 77; Chocolate Manufacturers of America, pp. 45,
74, 85, 87; Specialty Coffee Association of America, pp. 11, 27, 32, 50, 57; Tea Council of
the U.S.A., pp. 16, 61, 68.

Cover Photo: Tom Pantages

Contents

1

The History of Caffeine

If you asked a group of people sitting at a lunch counter or in a coffee shop what the most commonly used drug in America is, you might hear several answers. One person, thinking of illegal drugs, might say cocaine. Another, thinking of medications, might say aspirin. A third person could identify alcohol or nicotine as the most commonly abused legal substance. They would all be wrong.

Although it is not generally associated with the harmful effects of drug abuse, the most commonly taken drug in the United States, and possibly in the world, is caffeine.[1] Caffeine is a common ingredient in beverages such as coffee, tea, soft drinks, and cocoa. It is also in chocolate candy, chocolate ice cream, and other chocolate foods.[2] Caffeine is even an ingredient in some

common pain relievers. It can also be obtained in tablet form without a prescription.[3]

Many Americans start their day with a cup of coffee and may end their day with a cup after dinner. Coffee shops have become popular gathering places in recent years. Cola sodas are the most popular soft drinks in the United States and iced tea is quickly gaining in popularity. In order to avoid caffeine, you would either have to avoid all of these products or choose decaffeinated or caffeine-free versions of them.

The number of people who consume caffeine on a daily basis is quite large, but the way we consume it is changing. In 1962, three out of four Americans drank coffee—ounce for ounce the biggest source of caffeine—regularly.[4] Now, only about half of the country consumes coffee on a regular basis. However, more people are consuming soft drinks, or sodas, many of which contain caffeine. The percentage of people consuming soda is up from one person in three in 1962 to nearly six out of ten now. Tea, which also contains caffeine, is now consumed by about 30 percent of Americans.[5]

What is Caffeine?

Caffeine is a drug. A drug is any substance that changes how the body works. Caffeine has a stimulating effect on the brain and nerves, the heart and circulatory system, and the stomach and intestines. It also acts as a mild diuretic, which means that it helps increase urination and helps eliminate water from the body. Caffeine has advantages and disadvantages. When taken in small to moderate amounts, caffeine can be harmless and even beneficial. It makes people feel more alert, helps them concentrate, and helps them work longer. It is used as an ingredient in some pain

For many Americans, the day does not start without a cup of coffee and the morning paper.

relievers because it has been shown to help relieve headaches.[6] Caffeine is also found as an active ingredient in a variety of prescription drugs.[7]

The downside to caffeine is that too much of it can cause nervousness, anxiety, irritability, and a jittery feeling. It can interfere with a person's ability to get to sleep or to stay asleep.

Caffeine can also have some more serious side effects. It is known to raise blood pressure. It can also increase the number of times your heart beats each minute. The increase in blood pressure and heart rate is one reason that people feel nervous if they have had too much caffeine. Doctors frequently tell people who have high blood pressure or heart conditions to completely eliminate caffeine from their diet.

For women, taking in too much caffeine has been linked to infertility and, for pregnant women, to an increased chance of miscarrying during a pregnancy.[8]

Some studies have also shown a link between drinking coffee and an increased risk of cancer.[9]

For most people, however, the biggest concern caused by drinking coffee, tea, or colas, or eating too much chocolate is "jitters," the nervousness and agitation that can come from caffeine. The amount of coffee or other caffeine sources that brings on these symptoms is variable and is different for each individual. For some people, five or six mugs of coffee a day causes no problem. For others, even a little caffeine, say the amount in a chocolate bar, interferes with their sleep and perhaps makes their hands shake, giving them a nervous feeling.

Because of these health concerns, many people choose to avoid caffeine and either do not drink coffee, tea, or colas, or choose products that have had caffeine removed. Decaffeinated coffee, tea, and colas contain little caffeine. Caffeine-free products contain no caffeine. Both are now widely available. Other alternatives include herbal teas and some soft drinks such as seltzer, fruit-flavored soft drinks, or ginger ale, which have never contained caffeine.

Where Does Caffeine Come From?

Caffeine is found naturally in many plants, which is why it has been a common element in food and drink for centuries. The four largest plant sources of caffeine are the beans of the coffee plant; tea leaves; pods from the cocoa plant, from which chocolate is produced; and kola nuts, the flavoring ingredient in colas. Caffeine in other products is an added ingredient.

More than sixty-three plant species contain caffeine in their leaves, seeds, or fruits. So why do plants produce caffeine? Caffeine appears to help the plants grow by acting as a mild insecticide. It also appears to help protect the plants from infections by bacteria and fungi.

Coffee, tea, chocolate, and cola have long and interesting histories. They have risen and fallen in popularity but they have been a part of the human diet for a long time.

Coffee

Coffee is made from coffee beans, which are the berries of the coffee plant. Coffee plants originated in Africa and the Middle East, but are now grown in tropical countries around the world.[10] There are three species of coffee plants: *Coffea arabica, Coffea robusta,* and *Coffea liberica.* Most of the coffee used in the world comes from arabica coffee plants. Coffee plants grow best at higher altitudes, between two and seven thousand feet above

sea level, which is why some brands of coffee are advertised as being "mountain grown."

The first use of coffee is unknown but coffee beans, which are the berries of the coffee plant, were known to be chewed in Africa as early as A.D. 850 The story goes that a young Ethiopian man watching his family's goats noticed that the goats who ate red berries off the coffee plant were more playful and friskier. He started eating the berries, too, and experienced more energy.[11]

The use of coffee spread. At first the beans were simply eaten. Later they were steeped in wine and the wine was consumed. Coffee beans were soon roasted and ground and steeped in hot water to make a beverage. As the popularity of coffee grew, the plants were taken from Africa to southern Arabia and beyond. Coffee reached the Middle East in the 1200s. The word coffee comes from the Arab word *qahwah*, meaning "bitter water."[12]

Coffee drinking was introduced to Europe in the 1500s and to North America in the 1660s. Coffeehouses, which served as centers for business, cultural, and political life, were opened in the 1600s in London and thrived. They gave upper-class Europeans a place to visit and discuss the news of the day.[13] Coffeehouses actually served as places of business for large trading companies in London.[14]

Coffee had become so popular by the 1700s that Johann Sebastian Bach wrote his *Coffee Cantata* about a girl who loved to drink coffee. The cantata's lyrics show that, even at that time, people wondered about the health effects of drinking too much coffee.[15] Coffee is grown in many countries, including Brazil, Colombia, Ethiopia, Kenya, and Jamaica. Some high-quality coffee is grown in Hawaii, but the United States imports far more coffee than it grows.[16] Different countries grow different

Coffee beans grow in mountainous tropical regions. Countries like Brazil and Colombia are famous for their coffee.

varieties of coffee, which have variations in taste and some small variations in the amount of caffeine they contain. The amount of caffeine in different varieties of coffee beans ranges from 1.1 percent by weight to 1.42 percent by weight, which is not a huge difference.[17]

Differences in coffee flavor are also produced by the length of time the beans are roasted. Dark roast coffee is almost black, compared to lighter roasts that are medium to dark brown. The flavor of coffee can also be varied by added flavorings such as cinnamon, vanilla, cardamom, or almond extract.

Coffee may be consumed black or with milk or cream, and with or without sugar or artificial sweetener. Coffee with nothing added to it has very few calories, but additives such as cream and sugar can greatly increase the number of calories per cup.

In America, coffee can be bought as whole beans that can be ground at home, as ground coffee, or as powdered instant coffee. Instant coffee is made by brewing coffee and then extracting all of the water. This leaves a powder that makes a cup of coffee when water is added. Instant coffee is also available with dried milk, sweeteners, and flavorings added. Coffee may also be consumed as an iced beverage.

As a beverage, coffee is a mainstay of the American diet. Virtually every place that sells food, from the smallest fast food outlet to the finest gourmet restaurant, also sells coffee. Coffee is also a symbol of hospitality in the home. In many American homes, the first thing a visitor is offered is a cup of coffee.

Although coffee has been slipping in popularity in the United States, there is a trend upwards again as gourmet coffees become more widely available. Coffeehouses and shops that sell gourmet coffees have opened across the country.

Many coffee shops and restaurants now sell espresso and cappuccino, two variations on basic coffee. This trend started in the state of Washington, where such coffee concoctions have become popular enough to be sold in fast-food restaurants.

Espresso, which originated in Italy, is a strong black coffee made from coffee beans that have been roasted longer until they are black and glossy. Espresso is made using an espresso pot or espresso maker, which forces very hot water through very finely ground espresso coffee beans. A cup of espresso is small since it is intensely strong. It has more caffeine per ounce than regular coffee.[18] Many families have a special set of fine china espresso cups which are tiny, holding only one or two ounces of liquid. Traditionally, espresso is black, with perhaps some sugar or a twist of lemon peel. In the United States, a popular form of espresso is latté, which has steamed milk and perhaps a flavored syrup added.

Cappuccino is usually made from strong coffee—some restaurants use espresso—steamed milk, and a layer of frothed milk made by blowing steam into milk until it bubbles. First, the milk is steamed; next, the coffee is added; and then frothy milk is made and floated on top. In some coffeehouses, whipped cream takes the place of the frothy milk. Cinnamon or cocoa powder is then sprinkled on top. Pre-made cappuccino is also available in bottles and as a powdered instant drink.

Coffee is also used as a flavoring agent in foods such as coffee ice cream, frozen yogurt, candies, and cakes.

13

Tea

Tea has an even longer history than coffee, but unlike coffee, we know the name of its discoverer. The legend is that, in the year 2737 B.C., a Chinese emperor named Shen Nung was boiling water when leaves from a bush drifted into the pot. He drank the brew and discovered that it quenched his thirst, cheered him up, and enabled him to go with less sleep.[19] Five thousand years later, tea is still the national drink of China. In Chinese restaurants, the first thing served is traditionally a pot of tea.

Tea plants are native to China and India. They come from only one species of plants, *Camellia sinensis*. Tea plants are extremely hardy and long-lived. One tea plant in China is reported to be eighteen hundred years old.[20]

The drinking of tea spread to Japan around A.D. 600. Tea became so important to Japanese culture that the making of tea became a ceremony. Dutch traders brought the practice from East Asia over to Europe in the 1600s and to North America shortly after that.[21] Tea was soon a common drink at coffeehouses in England, a country that still celebrates its daily teatime at 4:00 P.M., when everyone stops what they are doing to have a cup of tea.

Tea played a role in the American Revolution. In 1767, England placed a tax on all tea used in the American colonies. The colonists revolted and refused to drink tea, switching to herbal drinks, cocoa or hot chocolate, and coffee. In 1773, a group of Bostonians dressed up as Native Americans and raided a British ship in Boston Harbor, throwing all its shipment of tea overboard. This event is called the Boston Tea Party and was an early act of defiance by Americans against Britain.[22]

America made two contributions to the world of tea in 1904. That year brought about the invention of the tea bag, which made brewing a cup of tea easy and neat, and the creation of iced tea, which is still a popular beverage. Powdered instant tea was invented in 1948.[23]

Tea comes in three common forms: black tea (the most common form in the United States), oolong tea, and green tea. All three varieties are made from the tea plant by treating the leaves differently. For black tea, the leaves are fermented, or allowed to break down, before they are dried. Oolong tea is partially fermented, while green tea is steamed and then dried without fermentation.[24] Teas such as Earl Grey are black teas with spices or flavorings added.

A confusing fact is that almost any beverage made from steeping leaves or other parts of plants in boiling water is called a tea. However, there is only one plant that can specifically be called tea. There are many beverages made from plants such as chamomile, peppermint, spearmint, and hibiscus. These are herbal teas and most do not contain caffeine and have nothing to do with the plant known as tea. There are also tea mixtures that contain tea leaves blended with herbs which may contain some or no caffeine. Decaffeinated tea leaves in bags and decaffeinated iced teas are also available.

In the past few years, pre-made iced tea has become widely popular in the United States. These teas can be bought sweetened or unsweetened, with or without lemon or other flavorings, and are available with caffeine or decaffeinated.

Like coffee, tea can be consumed black, with nothing added to it. It can also be consumed with milk, sweetener, or both added, or with a little lemon juice and sweetener added. In

All three forms of tea—black, oolong, and green—are made from the same tea plant, such as the one shown here.

addition to sugar and artificial sweetener, honey can also be used to sweeten tea.

Chocolate

Unlike coffee and tea, chocolate is available primarily as a food rather than a beverage. As a beverage, it is available as cocoa and hot chocolate, and as chocolate milk. As a food, chocolate is available as an ingredient in cakes, ice cream, cookies, and other treats such as chocolate candy and fudge. The source of chocolate is the cocoa beans from the cocoa or cacao tree, which grows in tropical countries near the equator.[25] The Latin name for the plant is *Theobroma cacao.*

Like coffee and tea, the use of cocoa beans (also called cacao beans) goes back many years. They were known to be roasted and turned into a drink by the three ancient civilizations of Central and South America—the Mayas, Toltecs, and Aztecs—as early as 1000 B.C.[26]

Unlike modern hot chocolate or cocoa drinks, ancient chocolate was a bitter drink that was used in religious ceremonies.[27] The Aztecs believed cocoa beans were a gift from the gods. The word cacao, from which we get cocoa, is Mayan for "bitter juice" and the word chocolate comes from the Mayan for "sour water."[28] Cocoa beans were so important in Central American life that they were used as money.

Christopher Columbus was served a chocolate beverage during one of his trips to the Western Hemisphere, but he found it bitter and unpleasant.[29] In 1519, the explorer Hernando Cortés met with the Aztecs of Mexico. The Aztecs flavored their chocolate drink with honey, spices, and vanilla, to make it tastier, and Cortés was more impressed with it. He brought chocolate to Europe where it was served as a sweet hot drink for anyone rich enough to afford it.[30] Europeans were drinking chocolate before they consumed either tea or coffee.

Chocolate could be found only in beverages until the early 1800s. Then the Dutch learned how to create cocoa powder from cocoa beans. An English firm discovered how to make a dark solid chocolate from cocoa beans, which could be eaten. A few years later, milk chocolate was invented.

To make chocolate and cocoa powder, the nibs or meat of cocoa beans are roasted and ground up to create chocolate liquor, a fluid from which cocoa butter (which is also used in skin-care products such as suntan lotions) and cocoa powder are made. Chocolate liquor can be cooled and molded into blocks for use in baking or cooking or can be sweetened and made into eating chocolate. Eating chocolate comes in several forms, such as semisweet chocolate (also called dark chocolate) and milk chocolate, which is a lighter color. Milk chocolate contains extra cocoa butter and milk or cream.[31]

Not everything that is chocolate flavored has real chocolate in it. Many chocolate-flavored candies or cakes may have the words "artificially flavored" somewhere on the label, which means they contain no real chocolate.

Chocolate contains very little caffeine compared to coffee or tea. The amount of caffeine in a cup of hot cocoa is very small when compared to the amount in coffee. However, chocolate also contains small amounts of two chemicals, called theobromine and theophylline, which are active in the body and act similarly to caffeine. Different types of chocolate and brands of chocolate candy bars vary in amounts of caffeine.

Cola

The kola nut is the most recent of the common sources of caffeine in the United States. Kola nuts are one of the flavoring ingredients in cola sodas. The nuts come from two species of evergreen tree, *Cola acuminata* and *Cola nitida*, which are native to West Africa. In Africa, the nuts are chewed like gum.[32]

Cola soft drinks rank second to coffee as a source of caffeine in the United States. Like cocoa beans, kola nuts also contain small amounts of theobromine.

Carbonated soft drinks—the name was used to separate them from hard liquor drinks such as whiskey—were first manufactured in America in the early 1800s and the fizzy drinks were said to be healthy and beneficial.[33] Pharmacists frequently created these drinks from such ingredients as local roots, herbs, and other flavorings, adding carbonated water to make the fizz.

Root beer had already been made for some time on a small scale, by bar owners and local brewers who sold it along with their alcoholic beers and ales. Root beer was first made in large enough quantities to be shipped to other locations in the 1870s. The first cola soft drink was created in Georgia in the 1880s by a pharmacist. He used coca leaves, kola nuts, citrus, cinnamon, and other flavorings in his creation of a syrup. He sold the syrup and also mixed it with water in the soda fountain area of his pharmacy. Originally, cola was made from cola syrup mixed with plain water and was not carbonated. Someone tried mixing the syrup with carbonated water and the first great soft drink was born.

After the success of the first cola mix, other brands came along that vary the cola flavoring formula slightly. Other people

The Amount of Caffeine in Soft Drinks
(in milligrams)

Soft Drink Brand	Per 12-Ounce Can	Per Ounce
JOLT COLA™	72	6
GATORADE SUN-BOLT (11.6 OZ.)™	58	5
MOUNTAIN DEW™ *	55	4.58
DIET MOUNTAIN DEW™ *	55	4.58
MELLO YELLOW™ *	52.8	4.4
TAB™	46.8	3.9
COCA-COLA™	46.5	3.87
DIET COKE™	46.5	3.87
SHASTA COLA™	44.4	3.7
SHASTA CHERRY COLA™	44.4	3.7
SHASTA DIET COLA™	44.4	3.7
MR. PIBB™	40.8	3.4
SUGAR-FREE MR. PIBB™	40.8	3.4
OK SODA™	40.5	3.37
DR. PEPPER™	39.6	3.3
PEPSI-COLA™	37	3.08
DIET PEPSI-COLA™	36	3
RC COLA™	36	3
DIET RC COLA™	36	3
DIET RITE COLA™	36	3
CHERRY SPICE SLICE™	35	2.91
DR. SLICE™	35	2.91
SLICE RED™	34	2.83
SLICE COLA™	11	.91
7 UP™	0	0
GINGER ALE (all brands)	0	0

* These brands contain no caffeine in Canada.
Source: Soda manufacturers and Institute of Food Technologists, April 1983, based on data from the National Soft Drink Association.

also created other soft drinks, called pepper drinks, that are similar to cola. These drinks also contain caffeine.

Although kola nuts are one source of caffeine in cola, additional amounts of caffeine are added. Caffeine is also added to some citrus-flavored soft drinks and to some brands of root beer.

One reason caffeine is added to soft drinks is for its bitter taste, which is why caffeine-free colas may not taste exactly the same as caffeinated cola.

Decaffeination

Coffee and tea come in decaffeinated varieties. Decaffeination is the process of removing caffeine from products that contain it. Caffeine-free sodas do not have caffeine as an added ingredient.

For coffee and tea, there are three common ways to remove the caffeine: the direct method, the water method, and the carbon dioxide method. The direct method uses a chemical called methylene chloride as a solvent. Green coffee beans or moistened tea leaves are treated with methylene chloride, which dissolves their caffeine. Then the beans are steamed to remove the methylene chloride. Later the caffeine can be removed from the methylene chloride for use in medications, soft drinks, and caffeine tablets.[34]

A variation of this method uses water to remove caffeine, along with other flavoring chemicals, from steamed coffee beans or tea leaves. Then the caffeine is removed from the water, using methylene chloride, and the water is added back to restore some of the flavor to the treated coffee beans or tea leaves. The beans are then steamed to remove any methylene chloride that may have been added back with the decaffeinated water. This process results in a more flavorful product.

Methylene chloride is known to cause cancer in animals when they inhale it. However, when laboratory animals drink diluted methylene chloride in water, which is more like humans drinking coffee, they do not develop cancer. The United States Food and Drug Administration has examined decaffeinated coffee and determined that so little methylene chloride is left in the final product made using the direct method that the risk of developing cancer is very remote. More methylene chloride is found in the air on a smoggy day than in decaffeinated coffee.[35] However, because of the possibility of a link between methylene chloride and cancer, some coffee and tea producers have switched to either the water method or carbon dioxide method of decaffeination.

The newest of the three methods of decaffeination uses carbon dioxide to remove caffeine. It is superior to the water method in that it leaves in more coffee or tea flavor.

The caffeine that is removed from coffee and tea is not thrown away. Some of it is used in medications and as added caffeine in colas and other sodas. Some is converted to theophylline, which is used as a medication to treat lung problems such as asthma and emphysema.[36]

Although people tend to talk of decaffeinated coffee and tea as if they had no caffeine, decaffeination actually removes only about 97 percent of the caffeine.[37] For most people, the tiny amount of caffeine left in a cup of decaffeinated coffee is unnoticeable.

Questions for Discussion

1. Caffeine is the most widely used drug in the world. Why do people not recognize it as a drug? Why do you think caffeine use is generally accepted? How does caffeine differ from dangerous drugs that are abused?

2. Coffee, tea, and kola nuts all grow in tropical climates and do not grow in the mainland United States. Name another food product that must be imported into the country from the tropics.

3. In England, people have tea at 4:00 P.M. every day just the way Americans have a coffee break. Can you think of any other foods associated with a rest break?

Physical Effects of Caffeine

Chemically, caffeine is one of a class of drugs called methylxan-thines.[1] It is odorless and has a slightly bitter taste in its pure form. As a drug, caffeine is considered a stimulant because it stimulates the central nervous system. It is also called a psychoactive drug because it can alter a person's mood and change his or her behavior.

As discussed, the most common food sources of caffeine for Americans are coffee beans, kola nuts, tea leaves, and cocoa beans.[2] In South America, caffeine is also found in the leaves of the maté plant and in guarana seeds. South Americans make a hot beverage from maté leaves, called yerba maté. Guarana seeds can be made into a paste which is then made into a hot beverage and a soda. Maté leaves do not contain large amounts of caffeine, but guarana seeds are a potent source of the drug, containing

4 percent caffeine by weight compared to 1 to 1.5 percent for coffee.[3] Maté tea can be found in some health food stores and guarana soda is sold in stores that specialize in South American foods.

All caffeine is the same, whether the source is coffee, tea, or other products and whether the product is a food or a beverage. The caffeine found in tea was once called theine before it was understood that it was the exact same chemical as the stimulant found in coffee.[4]

Many of the plants that produce caffeine also produce small amounts of other drugs that have stimulatory effects, such as theophylline and theobromine, both of which are also methylxanthine drugs. Theophylline is commonly used as a prescription drug to treat lung conditions such as asthma and emphysema, since it has a strong stimulatory effect on the lungs. Theobromine is also a stimulant like caffeine but is much weaker. It is found in much greater quantities in cocoa beans than is caffeine, and a portion of the stimulant effect of chocolate and cocoa is actually due to theobromine.

The Effects of Caffeine

Since caffeine is usually consumed in foods and beverages, it enters the body through the intestinal system. A solution of purified caffeine can be injected into the bloodstream directly using a hypodermic needle. Injections of caffeine are occasionally used for medical purposes but the vast majority of people get their caffeine from foods and beverages. Because it is water soluble, caffeine passes easily from the intestines into the blood and then is circulated through the body.

The coffee plant is an evergreen that produces berries that contain the coffee beans. As the berries ripen, they turn red.

Caffeine is metabolized, or broken down, into other chemicals in the liver. Your liver breaks caffeine into several chemicals, or metabolites, including theophylline and theobromine, and these chemicals are then eventually processed through the kidneys and leave the body in the urine. These chemicals, notably theophylline and theobromine, also act as stimulants in the body.[5]

In your body, caffeine interrupts the action of a chemical called adenosine. Adenosine is a neurotransmitter. This means it is a chemical that helps transmit signals from one nerve to another. Adenosine is active in the heart, blood vessels, gastrointestinal system and other parts of the body, controlling activities such as heart rate, blood pressure, and the ability to fall asleep. Adenosine and caffeine have similar chemical structures. In the body, caffeine binds with some of the chemicals that are supposed to bind with adenosine. When caffeine is bound in place of adenosine, adenosine's actions in the body are interrupted. It is caffeine's interference with the action of adenosine that causes its effect on the body.[6]

Alcohol slows the breakdown of caffeine in the liver, increasing the length of time caffeine stays in the body. Smoking tobacco speeds up caffeine's breakdown, shortening the time it is in the body.[7]

The peak effect of caffeine occurs about thirty to sixty minutes after something with caffeine in it is consumed.[8] Caffeine stays in the body for several hours as it slowly breaks down. It has a half-life of three to seven hours. This means that half of the amount of caffeine in you is broken down and eliminated in that time and half of what is left is eliminated over the same number of hours. This pattern continues until the caffeine is completely eliminated. So, the effects of caffeine diminish relatively quickly but small amounts linger in your body for some time.[9]

How caffeine affects you varies with how much you take in, how fast your body breaks it down, and whether or not you use it regularly. There are many factors that affect how caffeine acts on a given person. A 150-milligram dose of caffeine in a strong cup of coffee will affect a person more than 50 milligrams from a cup of tea. Two people drinking a cup of coffee from the same pot may be affected differently if one person breaks down caffeine faster than the other. A person who never consumes coffee will react to one cup of coffee far more than someone who consumes five cups a day because he or she is not used to caffeine. The person with a five-cup-a-day habit does not respond to small amounts of caffeine because his or her body has learned to tolerate the drug.[10] All of these factors mean that no two people may react to caffeine the same way.

Because the effects of caffeine depend on the size of the dose, your body size also plays a role. If you weigh 100 pounds, 100 milligrams of caffeine is one milligram per pound for you. If you weigh 200 pounds, the same dose is half a milligram per pound and will probably have half the effect.

Caffeine affects the central nervous system (the brain and nerves), the heart and circulation, the lungs, the intestinal system, the muscles, the kidneys and urinary tract, and the reproductive system. In most of these body parts, caffeine acts as a stimulant.

The Brain and the Nervous System. The main reason most people use caffeine is to help them wake up and give them

a feeling of alertness. It has these effects because it stimulates the central nervous system.

However, the alertness obtained from a little coffee becomes nervousness and anxiety when you drink too much. The wake-up call of a morning cup of tea becomes tossing and turning if you drink two cups of tea before going to bed. In general, the more caffeine a person drinks, the more likely that person is to suffer these side effects.

Because caffeine affects the brain and nerves, it can affect your mood, but the effect it has varies from person to person and with the amount you take. A small to moderate amount of caffeine elevates the mood, possibly as a result of reducing fatigue. On the other hand, too much caffeine causes jitters, irritability, light-headedness, anxiety, and nervousness.[11] Taking in a higher amount of caffeine than usual will frequently lead to a feeling of agitation, including shaky hands and anxiety.

It is no secret that caffeine can interrupt sleep patterns, causing sleeplessness or interrupted sleep. Drinking a cup of coffee before bedtime will also cause insomnia, the inability to fall asleep, in some people. Most people who drink a cup of coffee before bedtime will take longer to fall asleep and may wake up more frequently during the night. In general, people who consume a lot of caffeine sleep less than people who do not.

Because caffeine increases alertness, many people assume that a cup of coffee will help sober up someone who is drunk. This is a myth. Caffeine does not counteract the effects of alcohol. Giving a drunk person coffee simply means you will have a wide-awake drunk.

Heart and Circulatory System. Some of the jitters caused by too much caffeine are due to its effects on the heart and circulatory system.[12] High doses of caffeine can increase the heart rate (the number of heartbeats per minute). The heart is stimulated to beat faster and harder by caffeine, especially in people who are not used to it. Because of this effect, it was once feared that caffeine could trigger a heart attack. Almost all medical studies of caffeine and heart attacks show there is little or no relationship between the two.[13]

Caffeine also raises blood pressure a little in some people, especially in those who are not used to it. This small increase in blood pressure is reduced or may be less noticeable in people who regularly use caffeine.

Some studies have also shown that drinking coffee can increase levels of cholesterol in the blood. However, the main studies that link coffee and high cholesterol were done in Sweden, where they make coffee by boiling ground coffee in water without filtering it. Coffee made this way contains more oils from the coffee beans than does drip coffee or even percolated coffee, which may make a difference. Most studies that look at American-style coffee have not found any association between coffee and higher cholesterol levels.[14]

Lungs. In the same way that caffeine can increase the heart rate, it also increases your breathing rate. When caffeine is broken down in the body, it becomes theophylline. Theophylline is known to help people with breathing problems. A cup of coffee may help someone who has asthma or other breathing difficulties, but it should not be used or relied on in the same way as medications that are specially prescribed for these problems.

Muscles. In addition to reducing tiredness and increasing alertness, caffeine helps increase the amount of work the muscles

Coffee berries are shown here being picked by hand.

can do. Caffeine gives a person a quicker reaction time than he or she would have without caffeine.[15] It is known to improve athletic performance, which is why caffeine is considered a performance enhancer by the U.S. Olympic Committee. The improvement is strictly due to increased endurance. In other words, caffeine can make an athlete run longer, but not faster, so that it may help a marathon runner, but not a sprinter.

Olympic athletes undergo drug testing to screen out drugs that enhance athletic performance. Caffeine is allowable in small to moderate amounts but too much caffeine in the blood—more than that in a few cups of coffee—can cause an athlete to be disqualified from the Olympic Games and other international competitions.[16] Caffeine interferes with fine coordination of the muscles, however. Too much caffeine can make the hands and fingers shake visibly, interfering with such tasks as fine sewing or handwriting. Most people will not notice this effect until they have consumed several cups of coffee, but people who must do extremely delicate work may notice tiny amounts of shaking in their hands. Eye surgeons and fine artists frequently avoid caffeine, to keep their hands from shaking even slightly. Champion sharpshooters frequently avoid caffeine because it affects their steadiness and their aim.

Intestinal System. The intestinal system also reacts to caffeine. Too much caffeine can cause diarrhea because it speeds the action of the lower intestine.[17] It can also increase the amount of acid that the stomach produces.[18] For some people, drinking too much coffee causes upset stomachs or acid indigestion. People with ulcers or other stomach or intestinal irritations are usually told by their physicians to cut caffeine out of their diets.

Reproductive System. Studies of the effects of caffeine on women have been confusing. Some medical studies link caffeine use to fibrocystic disease and problems with fertility while other studies show no link. Although some scientific studies have shown an increased risk of birth defects in animals that have been fed very large amounts of caffeine, studies of women who drink caffeine have not shown any such link.[19]

Several years ago, a few medical studies reported that women who used caffeine were more likely to develop fibrocystic disease. In fibrocystic disease, the breast contains noncancerous lumps. Recent studies have failed to show any direct relationship between fibrocystic disease and the amount of caffeine a woman consumes.[20] However, women with fibrocystic breast disease are still often told to avoid caffeine.

There have also been some worries that caffeine intake during pregnancy can cause birth defects. When pregnant laboratory rats were fed large amounts of caffeine all at one time, they gave birth to some offspring that were missing some toes. However, other studies of rats that were given even higher amounts of caffeine had no birth defects. One study that showed that laboratory animals suffered delayed bone development if their mothers were given caffeine also showed that this delay was temporary and reversed itself on its own.[21]

When large numbers of pregnant women—some of whom drank coffee and some of whom didn't—were studied, it was found that women who drank coffee regularly were more likely to have babies with lower birth weights than were women who did not drink coffee.[22]

More recently, studies about miscarriages and caffeine were published. These studies were conflicting and as such unable to find a definite link between heavy caffeine use and miscarriage. However, it is something to consider.[23]

The bottom line is that women who are pregnant or trying to become pregnant may choose to limit their caffeine intake. In 1980, the United States Food and Drug Administration (FDA) advised pregnant women to limit their intake of caffeine or avoid it altogether. The FDA has not changed its position and the advice still stands.

Another thing that expectant mothers must remember is that what goes into their bloodstream goes into their unborn child's bloodstream also. Mothers who drink large amounts of caffeine may give birth to babies that show signs of caffeine jitters. Caffeine is also present in the breast milk of mothers who drink tea or coffee. Breast milk can contain half the amount of caffeine that is in the mother's bloodstream, which means she may be giving her baby a dose of caffeine with each feeding.[24]

Caffeine and Cancer

Several times over the last twenty years, the use of caffeine has been linked with an increased risk of developing cancer. However, for every scientific study that shows that there might be a link other studies show no link.

Cancer occurs when a group of cells in the body start to grow wildly and in an uncontrolled fashion. These growths may cause illness or death if they interfere with your body's organs. Some cancers are also deadly because they spread throughout the body. Cancer is caused by a change in the genetic structure of a cell that causes it to grow and divide abnormally. Caffeine has been thought to cause certain types of cancer but many studies of caffeine and cancer have produced contradictory results.

35

Caffeine is known to change the cells of bacteria, insects, plants, and humans in the laboratory. But such findings do not necessarily mean that caffeine will cause cancer in humans.

The most serious cancer link to coffee comes from one study reported in 1981 that showed people who drank coffee had an increased risk of developing pancreatic cancer. Since then, many studies have been performed looking for any increased risk of cancer and only one other study has shown such a link. One very large study, in which medical researchers studied twenty-five thousand people, found no link between coffee drinking and a variety of common cancers. The enormous size of the study— very few medical studies evaluate that many people—means that the link between coffee and cancer is probably remote.[25]

Caffeine and Disease

Up until now, we've been discussing the intake of caffeine by people who are basically healthy. However, many people may have medical conditions that may be made worse by caffeine. They should consult their doctor. For many health problems, cutting back on caffeine makes sense. It is common sense for someone who has high blood pressure to limit a drug like caffeine that can raise blood pressure even further. Similarly, someone with an ulcer needs to consider the facts that caffeine increases stomach acid and that coffee irritates the stomach lining.

People who are diabetic or who have hypoglycemia (low blood sugar) may be told to eliminate caffeine or cut back on its use by their doctors. Caffeine speeds up metabolism a bit while it is in the bloodstream. Boosting the metabolism changes the levels of glucose (blood sugar) unpredictably.

In other cases, caffeine should be avoided because it might interfere with medications some people take to treat their condition. Caffeine does not mix well with several prescription drugs, notably birth control pills, some heart medications, tranquilizers, decongestants, and a group of drugs called monoamine oxidase inhibitors that are used to treat depression.

Some of these medications, including birth control pills and a heart medication called Verapamil™, slow down the metabolism of caffeine. This causes the effects of caffeine to last longer. This means that a lower-than-usual amount of caffeine can cause side effects such as insomnia, jitters, or irritability.

Other stimulants, such as decongestants, act similarly to caffeine, creating more of the same side effects. It is usually wise for someone who drinks a lot of coffee or other caffeinated beverages to tell their doctor this when they receive a prescription for any medications.

How Much Caffeine Is in That Cup?

Because caffeine is a plant product, the amount of caffeine in a food that naturally contains caffeine may depend on several factors. Caffeine amounts in food vary a great deal. They depend on the variety of the plant being used, the size of a serving, and the way it is prepared.[26] Some varieties of tea and of coffee beans have slightly more caffeine than others. Tea that is brewed longer has more caffeine than weak tea, just as espresso coffee has more caffeine than coffee prepared by the drip method, which has more caffeine than percolated coffee.

Colas and other beverages with caffeine have a more consistent percentage of caffeine. Although kola nuts are a natural source of caffeine, most of the caffeine in cola is added to

the final product. The caffeine is added as a bitter flavoring to balance out the sweetness of the other flavors in cola. Caffeine is also added to some fruit-flavored "energy" drinks.

When caffeine is an added ingredient, it is listed on the product label. It may be listed only in the fine print of the list of ingredients. When caffeine is not an added ingredient but part of the natural contents of another ingredient, it may not be listed. In other words, a can of cola has caffeine listed in its ingredients because caffeine was added. A bottle of iced tea does not always list caffeine, since caffeine is a natural part of tea. Decaffeinated coffees and teas are usually labeled as decaffeinated. Some products such as ginger ale that have never had caffeine may say so in large letters on the label as a selling point.

For most Americans, the largest single source of caffeine on an ounce-for-ounce basis is coffee. Coffee contains a more concentrated dose of caffeine than tea or other beverages and has much more caffeine than chocolate.

Most people measure the amount of coffee they drink by the cup. Unfortunately, not everyone agrees on a standard cup size. A standard cup measurement is eight ounces, but a fancy china coffee cup may hold about a five-ounce serving of coffee and a stoneware coffee mug can hold anywhere up to sixteen ounces. Most paper or plastic coffee cups at fast-food restaurants and coffee shops come in small, medium, and large. These can range in size from eight ounces to twenty-four ounces. A cup of espresso coffee, often called a demitasse cup ("half cup" in French), usually contains only one to two ounces.

If the size of a cup of coffee is confusing, the strength of coffee is even more confusing. Coffee varies greatly in the amount of caffeine it contains, depending on how it is prepared.

The Amount of Caffeine in Coffee
(in milligrams)

Type of Coffee	Per 5-Ounce Cup (range)	Average	Average per Ounce
DRIP METHOD	60-180	115	23
PERCOLATED	40-170	80	16
INSTANT	30-120	65	13
ESPRESSO	100*		100
DECAFFEINATED BREWED	2-5	3	0.6
DECAFFEINATED INSTANT	1-5	2	0.4

* Caffeine content in a one-ounce serving.
Source: U.S. Food and Drug Administration, Food Additive Chemistry Evaluation Branch.

Coffee made by the drip method, in which extremely hot water drips through ground coffee into a cup or carafe, is usually strongest. A five-ounce serving of drip coffee may contain between 60 and 180 milligrams of caffeine. Coffee prepared using the percolator method is slightly weaker, with a five-ounce serving containing between 40 and 170 milligrams. Instant coffee is weaker still, with between 30 and 120 milligrams of coffee in five ounces.[27] Espresso, a very strong form of black coffee, contains about 100 milligrams of caffeine in a one ounce serving.

Caffeine content varies with the way the coffee is made because hotter water removes more caffeine from the ground coffee. Espresso is made by forcing boiling water through finely ground coffee while drip coffee is made with water that is very hot but not boiling.

Although most of the caffeine is taken out of decaffeinated coffee, there is a small amount left. A five-ounce cup of decaffeinated coffee made from ground beans may contain 2 to 5 milligrams of caffeine. Instant decaffeinated coffee may contain 1 to 5 milligrams of caffeine in five ounces.[28]

Tea has slightly less caffeine per ounce than coffee. A five-ounce cup of brewed tea contains between 20 and 90 milligrams of caffeine. Some brands of tea are stronger, producing between 25 and 110 milligrams of caffeine in five ounces. Instant tea contains between 25 and 50 milligrams in five ounces. A twelve-ounce glass of iced tea contains between 67 and 76 milligrams of caffeine.[29]

These figures are reported by the United States Food and Drug Administration and are based on beverages prepared under laboratory settings from precisely measured amounts of coffee or

The Amount of Caffeine in Tea
(in milligrams)

Type of Tea	Per 5-Ounce Cup (range)	Average	Average per Ounce
BREWED (U.S.)	20-90	40	8
BREWED (IMPORTED)	25-110	60	12
INSTANT	25-50	30	6
ICED	67-76*	70	14

* Caffeine content in a twelve-ounce serving.
Source: U.S. Food and Drug Administration, Food Additive
Chemistry Evaluation Branch.

tea. Other published lists of caffeine amounts in coffee and tea give different results and use different cup sizes.

The amount of caffeine in a cup of coffee varies because people make and enjoy coffee at different strengths. In general, recipes for coffee call for using one to two tablespoons of ground coffee for each six-ounce cup of coffee. Naturally, using one tablespoon of ground beans yields a weaker brew both in taste and caffeine than using two tablespoons.

With tea, the amount of caffeine can be varied by letting the tea leaves brew or steep longer. Accidental mismeasurement is less of a variable with tea, since tea bags come premeasured. However, loose tea is available and you can make a stronger cup by using more tea.

Another confusing factor is milk. Some people pour four ounces of coffee into their cup and then add two ounces of milk, diluting the coffee by about 33 percent. People who add milk to tea similarly dilute the caffeine.

Because of all these variables, it is quite probable that no two people make coffee or tea the exact same strength. Even people who are drinking coffee from the same pot may not get the same amount of caffeine. If your parents make a pot of coffee in the morning and your father fills a ten-ounce mug and just adds sugar and your mother uses a six-ounce china cup and pours in some milk, they each drank a very different amount of caffeine. Add to this the facts that your father and mother do not weigh the same and may metabolize caffeine at different rates.

The amount of caffeine in soft drinks is less variable because caffeine is an added ingredient. Because the amount of caffeine soft-drink manufacturers use varies with their recipes, caffeine amounts in colas range from 11 to 72 milligrams per twelve-ounce can. The two major brands of cola contain a little less than the caffeine equivalent of about half a cup of coffee. Two non-cola soft drinks, both citrus-flavored sodas, contain slightly more caffeine per ounce than cola except in Canada, where they are caffeine-free.

Chocolate is not a major source of caffeine. Solid chocolate is a greater source of caffeine than chocolate drinks, but you would have to eat four or five chocolate bars to get the amount of caffeine contained in a cup of coffee. A one-ounce square of unsweetened baking chocolate contains 25 milligrams of caffeine. A one-ounce piece of chocolate contains 15 milligrams of caffeine, while three heaping tablespoons of cocoa mix contain 8 milligrams. A glass of chocolate milk made with two tablespoons of chocolate syrup contains 5 milligrams of caffeine.

However, chocolate contains considerable amounts of theobromine, which is a stimulant and which acts similarly to caffeine but is much weaker.[30] Theobromine has about one tenth the stimulating effect of caffeine. Chocolate also contains small amounts of theophylline, which is a stronger stimulant. The combination of caffeine, theobromine, and theophylline mean that you get a bigger stimulant "kick" from chocolate than would be predicted by just looking at the caffeine content. The caffeine-like effects of chocolate could be significant in someone who is also getting a lot of caffeine from other sources.[31]

A bar of chocolate contains between 68 and 314 milligrams of theobromine. A five-ounce cup of hot cocoa contains between 40 and 80 milligrams of theobromine.[32]

Caffeine is also found in several nonprescription and prescription pain relievers, diet aids, appetite suppressants, and stimulants. Caffeine contents in nonprescription medications may range from only a few milligrams to amounts equaling that in a cup of coffee. Straight caffeine in tablet form is available under several brand names. These products range from 100 milligrams to 200 milligrams per dose.

Caffeine tablets are often used as a "wake-up" by people who need to fight drowsiness or by those who work at night. College students have been known to use them when they need to stay up all night to study before exams. The potential for abuse is always present with caffeine tablets and they should be taken with caution.

In prescription strengths, caffeine is used as a central nervous system stimulant. It has been used to counteract overdoses of opiate drugs since opiates depress the central nervous system and caffeine stimulates it. Caffeine has also been used to treat breathing problems in infants.

Caffeine has been an ingredient in pain relievers for decades and ironically may have been added to help overcome headaches caused by caffeine withdrawal. In the late 1970s, the Food and Drug Administration found that caffeine was ineffective at helping to relieve pain. However, studies have since shown that caffeine does increase the effectiveness of pain relievers.[33] Many medications marketed for headaches, where the main active ingredient is aspirin or acetaminophen, contain caffeine.

Where people get their caffeine varies a bit with their age. Most young people get their caffeine in colas. Most older people get their daily caffeine in coffee. This pattern may be changing as coffee bars and coffeehouses selling gourmet coffees and beverages have become popular. In addition, iced tea in bottles has become widely available and specialty drinks such as cappuccino have become popular.

Chocolate comes in a variety of food products, from chocolate bars to cookies to hot beverages such as cocoa. Chocolate contains not only caffeine, but two other stimulants called theobromine and theophylline.

How Much Is Too Much?

The number of people who consume caffeine in some form is enormous and the number of people who have serious problems due to their caffeine use is relatively small. However, it is very possible—indeed it is easy—to overuse caffeine and even overdose on it.

In the United States today, the average daily intake of caffeine for children aged five to eighteen is about 38 milligrams. For adults, it is 200 milligrams.[34] That is the equivalent of a can of soda in children or about two cups of coffee in adults.

Those numbers are the average caffeine intake. Many adults and children take in no caffeine at all, while some adults take in amounts of caffeine that can be measured in grams rather than milligrams. Some of these people who take in large doses daily have no side effects. They get to sleep easily, don't feel nervous, and their hands do not shake. The ones with no side effects may be the exception and not the rule. Others have the side effects but do not stop drinking coffee, tea, or cola. They may not want to stop or they may feel they are unable to stop.

Caffeine can be fatal if you take in enough. Death by caffeine is extremely rare except in cases where someone has overdosed on caffeine tablets. In order to drink enough caffeine to cause death, you would have to ingest about 5,000 milligrams or 5 grams. In one case where a patient received an injection of caffeine by accident a dose of only 3,200 milligrams caused death.[35] Five grams of caffeine is the amount contained in fifty normal strength cups of coffee or about thirty-five strong cups of coffee. That large amount of coffee would have to be drunk rather quickly since the first doses of caffeine would be out of the system within a few hours.

It is possible to consume enough caffeine from coffee or tea to create severe health problems. The symptoms of a caffeine overdose are rapid and deep breathing (hyperventilation), very fast heart beat and uncoordinated twitching of the heart, convulsions, and imbalances in the amount of potassium, sugar, and other chemicals in the blood.[36]

Large amounts of caffeine can produce severe nervousness, anxiety, and insomnia. The side effects of too much caffeine can be confused with anxiety, neurosis, or other mental illnesses and can cause confusion.[37]

The amount that can cause these symptoms may be as small as 1,000 milligrams, the equivalent of eight or nine cups of coffee.

The overdose amount depends on such factors as a person's size, metabolism, and usual caffeine intake. A small person who never uses caffeine will react badly to a much smaller amount than will a large person who drinks three or four cups of coffee daily. The reasons for this difference are dependence and tolerance, two important aspects of caffeine use that will be covered in the next chapter.

Questions for Discussion

1. Why do you think the effects of caffeine vary so much from person to person?

2. If you wanted to lower your intake of caffeine, you might switch from drinking coffee to drinking tea. How much could you reduce your caffeine intake that way?

3. If you decided to switch from drinking caffeinated colas to decaffeinated colas, how difficult would it be for you? Can you buy decaffeinated cola where you usually buy soft drinks?

3

Is Caffeine Addictive?

The use of caffeine appears to be habit forming. However, most medical experts agree that caffeine is not seriously addictive, the way illegal drugs such as heroin or cocaine are. If drinking coffee and cola were merely habits created because these beverages are available and taste good, anyone who drank them regularly could switch to decaffeinated coffee or caffeine-free cola without a problem. But people who consume caffeine do notice a difference in the way they feel when they switch to decaffeinated beverages.

As with many drugs, two factors in the use and abuse of caffeine are dependence and tolerance.

Caffeine Dependence

Drug dependence occurs when your body has become accustomed to certain levels of a substance and does not function as

Berries are dried in the sun and split open to release the green coffee beans. The beans are sorted by hand. This is just the first step in the coffee-making process.

well when that level is not kept up. Dependence can be physical, psychological, or both.[1] Physical dependence occurs when the body needs a constant supply of the substance to keep from becoming ill from the lack of it. Psychological dependence occurs when a person craves the substance for the feeling of well-being it gives.

Caffeine is known to cause physical dependence. People who use caffeine regularly start to feel withdrawal symptoms such as headache, fatigue, and anxiety within a few hours if they go without it. People who give up caffeine also experience an intense desire for it. Because of that craving, it appears that caffeine causes psychological dependence as well.

The symptoms of caffeine withdrawal may be intense for people who quit cold turkey after using a lot of caffeine daily. Dr. Neal Benowitz has written, "Relief of withdrawal symptoms appears to be a substantial component of the satisfaction of coffee drinking, particularly the first cup of the day."[2]

A person can become caffeine dependent quite quickly, within a matter of several days or a couple of weeks of regularly drinking coffee, tea, or cola. Even drinking only a cup of coffee or one glass of cola each day can cause physical dependence on caffeine. This can be tested simply. If you usually drink a cola at lunch and dinner and then go without any caffeine for a few days you will probably be a bit tired and down or have a headache. The intensity of your withdrawal symptoms depends on how much caffeine you usually use and on how fast your body metabolizes caffeine.

A recent medical study evaluated daily caffeine use to see whether it caused a dependence syndrome. Medical researchers from Johns Hopkins University School of Medicine in Baltimore sought out people who thought they had a problem with caffeine and found sixteen such people. Some of these people had been advised to give up caffeine by their physician. One of these people used on average only 129 milligrams of caffeine daily while others drank more than 1,000 milligrams (one gram) a day. Interestingly, of the sixteen, only eight got their caffeine from coffee, the dietary source with the greatest concentration of caffeine. Seven got their caffeine in soft drinks and one drank tea as a caffeine source.[3]

The researchers questioned these people and asked them about their caffeine use. They learned that these people showed evidence of being dependent on caffeine. Several of the people involved in the study—including the person who only used an average of 129 milligrams a day (about one eight-ounce cup of coffee)—had been told to give up caffeine and had been unable to do it. Despite the fact that they wanted to cut back on caffeine and had tried, they had been unable to quit using it.

To evaluate physical dependence, the researchers asked eleven of these people to withdraw from all caffeine for two two-day periods. During these times, the people received either capsules containing their usual daily amount of caffeine or placebo capsules. This meant that the people spent two days without any caffeine and two days receiving the same amount of caffeine as they usually did, but did not know it. During each period, they were also questioned about their mood and asked to perform simple physical tasks such as pressing a button two hundred times quickly.

During the period when the people received no caffeine, nine of the eleven people reported symptoms of caffeine withdrawal. These symptoms included headaches, fatigue, depression, and failing to perform usual daily work or chores. Seven people reported suffering severe headaches. Two of these people made serious errors at work, one had to go to bed early, and one took a nap.

The researchers concluded that caffeine is a psychoactive drug that does create a dependence syndrome. They pointed out that the people who took part in the study were people who knew they drank too much coffee, soda, or tea.

The Johns Hopkins researchers said:

> *The volunteers for this study reported a variety of problems associated with their caffeine use, including arguments with family members and friends over their use, going to extremes to obtain caffeine-containing products, using them in potentially dangerous situations, and continuing to use them despite being told not to by a physician.*[4]

Caffeine Tolerance

Tolerance is the progressive decrease in the effectiveness of a drug. This means that if you drink, for example, a mug of coffee each morning your body has become used to that much caffeine each day and starts to ignore it. If you got some side effects of caffeine—jitteriness or an "up" feeling—when you first drank coffee, you no longer feel that. Now you get those feelings only if you drink more coffee than you usually do.

When a person starts to consume caffeine, he or she may feel jittery or notice mild shaking of the hands after a single dose. As a person starts using caffeine more regularly, this sensation is not noticed unless a second or third cup of coffee or perhaps a fourth can of cola is consumed.

A little caffeine has a much larger effect on someone who never uses caffeine because of the effects of tolerance. Someone who usually abstains from caffeine is more likely to feel the negative side effects of caffeine, the nervousness and anxiety, than someone who is used to caffeine.[5]

Tolerance to caffeine may be the single biggest reason different people react differently to the same amount of caffeine. Studies have shown that people react to a given amount of caffeine more strongly after they have not had caffeine for several days.

Is Caffeine Addicting?

Because regular caffeine use creates both dependence and tolerance, it appears to be addictive. Drug addiction is basically the physical and psychological dependence on a drug.

In an article on caffeine in a medical journal, Dr. Neal Benowitz wrote:

> *The three major criteria for addiction liability are psychoactivity, drug-reinforced behavior, and compulsive use. That caffeine is psychoactive and that some people consume caffeine compulsively is clear. That caffeine reinforces its consumption has recently been demonstrated in people. . . . Minor criteria for addiction liability include the development of tolerance, physical dependence, and recurrent intense desire for the drug, all of which are characteristic of regular caffeine consumers. Thus, there is a group of coffee drinkers who appear to be addicted to caffeine, although the extent of caffeine addiction in the population is unknown.[6]*

People may say they drink only one cup of coffee, but how much is that? Different cups hold different amounts of a beverage. The small white cup in front is an espresso cup and holds about two to three ounces of liquid. The large cups in the back hold twelve ounces of liquid when filled to the brim.

Whether caffeine is addictive may hinge on the word addiction. For many people, addiction applies only to use of a drug that causes intoxication or "getting high." Caffeine may elevate the mood and relieve fatigue but it is not intoxicating. However, compulsive use of a drug may not necessarily involve trying to become high. Nicotine is considered addictive and does not intoxicate people. Only 10 percent of people who smoke are able to kick the habit easily and with no problems. Use of alcohol can be addicting, but only about 14 percent of people who consume alcoholic beverages become dependent on alcohol. Alcohol may be a better example of the type of dependence caffeine creates than nicotine, since only a small percentage of the large number of people who consume caffeine develop a dependence on it and are unable to stop using it.

Caffeine is also not considered a "gateway" drug, one that leads to the use of stronger drugs. Dr. Richard Glass has written: "No one should attempt to use the new findings about caffeine dependence to trivialize the tragic consequences caused by addiction to tobacco, alcohol, or other harmful substances."[7]

It is important to note that enormous numbers of people drink coffee, tea, and cola each day and have no problem with caffeine. Eight out of ten Americans use caffeine regularly, a far greater number of people than use nicotine or alcohol, two other legal and widely used drugs. Misuse of alcohol leads to one hundred thousand deaths each year in the United States. Alcohol withdrawal is physically difficult and can even be fatal in some situations. Nicotine use—smoking—causes four hundred thousand deaths each year in the United States and many people spend years unsuccessfully trying to quit smoking.[8]

Though eight out of ten Americans use caffeine regularly, it is not considered a gateway drug. Here, green coffee beans are passed on a conveyor belt through a roaster.

Caffeine Withdrawal

The primary symptoms of withdrawal from caffeine are headaches, fatigue, and drowsiness. The headaches may be quite severe but will usually respond well to pain relievers.

Withdrawing from caffeine appears to cause headaches because caffeine dilates or widens blood vessels somewhat. The body has been used to a certain amount of caffeine keeping the blood vessels open wider than usual and these vessels get narrower without the caffeine. This reduces blood flow, which creates something similar to a migraine headache. In fact, caffeine is added to many medications for headaches, especially migraine headaches, to widen blood vessels.

The other side effects of caffeine withdrawal—fatigue and drowsiness—are not as unpleasant and go away in time.

Someone who wants to stop consuming caffeine cold turkey might decide to choose a time when no important work needs to be done, such as during a vacation.

The bad news is that the symptoms of caffeine withdrawal can make you feel miserable for up to a week. The good news is that you do not have to go through withdrawal. There is no reason that you have to stop using caffeine all at once. Slowly reducing the use of caffeine over the course of two or three weeks will work and is a lot less unpleasant than withdrawal. Stopping all caffeine suddenly works for some people, but others give up and grab a coffee or a cola by the second or third day just to get rid of the headache.

Methods for gradually decreasing the use of caffeine, along with tips on decaffeinated or caffeine-free drinks, are in Chapter 4.

Questions for Discussion

1. If you use caffeine, do you think you are physically dependent on it?

2. Do you know anyone who has tried to quit using caffeine?

3. If you were to quit caffeine, how would you go about it? Would you quit cold turkey or gradually decrease the amount you use?

4

Social Aspects of Caffeine

Because caffeine is a legal and commonly used drug, the social aspects of its use are important. Many people start and end their day with coffee. In addition, although people may worry about caffeine in coffee and tea, they often forget about other sources of caffeine that they consume on a day-to-day basis. We talk about getting the "coffee jitters" but no one talks about the "cola jitters."

Most people who consume caffeine do not consider it a drug nor do they consider drinking coffee or cola to be drug use. As Dr. Richard Glass noted, "Many people have difficulty recognizing that commonly consumed and socially approved beverages such as alcoholic drinks, coffee, and tea contain psychoactive drugs."[1]

Tea leaves are picked by hand. The leaves used are the top bud and top two leaves at the end of each new shoot. Tea, coffee, and cola are all commonly used and socially approved sources of caffeine.

But caffeine is a psychoactive drug and it is a stimulant. Even if you do not have any problems when you use it, you should be aware of what problems—physical and social—can occur.

Because the use of caffeine is so widespread, the message we get from society is that it is safe. For the majority of people it is. However, caffeine may not be safe for everyone. Caffeine dependency can become a problem for people who regularly consume caffeinated foods and beverages. Some people who have developed a habit of consuming coffee or tea daily will show some signs of withdrawal if they stop suddenly. In reality, caffeine has physical effects that are not safe for everyone.

Caffeine and Young People

One area of concern is the use of caffeine by children and young adults. Most of the studies that have been done on caffeine have examined its effects in adults. Few studies of caffeine have been done on young people. Although most children and young adults in the United States do not drink coffee, many get caffeine from cola, tea, or chocolate. Some drink large enough amounts of cola or iced tea that they may drink more than 100 milligrams of caffeine daily. That is the amount of caffeine in about two twelve-ounce cans of cola soda.

A dose that size does not sound like much until you remember body size plays a role in the effect of caffeine on the body. A fifty-pound child taking in 100 milligrams a day is getting two milligrams per pound, a high dose per pound. That same amount of caffeine in a 150-pound adult is only 0.66 milligrams per pound.

Because of the difference in size, children and young adults who are drinking a bottle of iced tea, a cup of coffee, or two cans of cola are consuming enough caffeine to bring them near the levels where the adverse side effects of caffeine show up. They may be nervous, jittery, and over-stimulated from caffeine.

Except for newborn babies, children break down caffeine the same way adults do. Newborns do not break down caffeine in the liver but get rid of it through the kidneys, which is a slower process. This means that caffeine stays in the baby's body longer than it does in the bodies of older children and adults. Caffeine may have a half-life of up to eighty-five hours in a baby compared to only a few hours in adults.[2]

Babies whose mothers drank a lot of caffeine during their pregnancy may have quite a bit of caffeine in their bloodstream when they are born. These babies may receive more caffeine in breast milk, if their mothers breast-feed and continue to drink coffee or tea. Even small doses of caffeine in breast milk may accumulate because the baby eliminates it slowly. The combination of a constant caffeine dose from breast milk and slow elimination can mean an irritable baby with caffeine jitters.

It was once thought that caffeine caused hyperactivity in children. This is the reason most children traditionally are not given coffee. However, more recent studies have shown that for some children, caffeine may actually have a calming effect. Children with attention deficit disorder, a condition that makes some people overactive, impulsive, and unable to concentrate, are sometimes given doses of caffeine to calm them down. Other stimulants, such as amphetamines, which can cause side effects similar to those of caffeine in adults, also have a calming effect on some hyperactive children.[3]

One explanation for this is that such children are hyperactive because their nervous systems are naturally under-aroused. In

other words, they move around a lot, speak out, and are generally disruptive in class because they need to keep themselves from becoming lethargic or falling asleep. According to this theory, stimulant drugs provide this excitation of the nervous system, making the hyperactivity unnecessary.[4]

However, only a small percentage of children are hyperactive. The majority of children can become irritable, anxious, and restless if they eat or drink too much caffeine. Again, dosage plays a part here. A twelve-ounce glass of iced tea given to a fifty-pound child is three times the per-pound caffeine dose as the same glass of tea given to a 150-pound adult.

An added problem to be considered with caffeine and children is that most drinks that contain caffeine have very little or no nutritive value. There are no vitamins in a cup of coffee, and colas are little more than water, sugar, and caffeine. When young people are drinking soft drinks, iced tea, or coffee, they are not drinking low-fat milk—a valuable source of calcium and other minerals and vitamins—or fruit juice, which provides vitamin C and other vitamins. Even if young people drink diet soft drinks, they are filling up on the beverages and not getting any nutritional value. They may also feel full from soft drinks and not feel hungry at mealtimes. In other words, they are choosing empty calories over nutritional calories.

Who Should Avoid Caffeine?

Although moderate amounts of caffeine are safe for most people, not everyone is "most people." There are some individuals who are extremely sensitive to caffeine and who feel the bad side effects of the drug at far lower doses than other people do. Just as some people can drink three cups of coffee and drift off to sleep blissfully an hour later, there are those for whom even one cup of coffee sets their hands shaking and their nerves jumping.

There are people who react even to the tiny (up to 5 milligrams) doses of caffeine present in decaffeinated coffee. Likewise, some people cannot sleep well after eating only a handful of chocolates.

Anyone who has been told by their doctor that they should avoid caffeine, should avoid it, plain and simple. People who have had heart problems, diabetes or hypoglycemia, insomnia, or ulcers, and women who are trying to become pregnant or who are pregnant are usually told to avoid caffeine or cut down on their intake.

However, being told to avoid caffeine and being able to do it are two different things. Because of physical and psychological dependence, not everyone who has been told to cut out caffeine is either willing to do it or able to do it without help. Doctors are now realizing that some people need some advice on how to give up caffeine as well as some psychological support.[5]

How to Reduce Caffeine Intake

There are basically two ways to reduce or eliminate caffeine intake, suddenly or gradually. Quitting caffeine cold turkey has the advantage of speed. You can get through the physical withdrawal symptoms in a few days in most cases and after that you only have to make sure you don't slip back into using caffeine again.

First, it may be wise to determine the pattern of your caffeine use. Do you need a cup of coffee as a morning eye-opener? Do you drink only coffee or only cola? Do you drink sixteen ounces of coffee in the morning and then have nothing else with caffeine all day?

Understanding your own pattern of caffeine use will help you change that pattern. If you decide to cut back on caffeine and eliminate your morning cup of coffee but not the six cans of cola you drink during the rest of the day, you will not be working on the bulk of your caffeine intake.

Because the headaches, fatigue, and lethargy that accompany giving up caffeine can be severe, it is best to choose a convenient time to quit. Caffeine withdrawal will probably affect your mood, and the quality of your work may suffer. Try quitting caffeine when you are on a vacation rather than during a week you have midterm exams. A vacation week will also give you a break from your usually daily patterns and can allow you to change your caffeine-drinking patterns more easily.

However, withdrawal is easier to talk about than to live through. Cutting back on caffeine gradually can work just as well as stopping suddenly, and may be a great deal more pleasant.

One way to cut back gradually would be to slowly drink fewer caffeinated beverages. If you drink several cans of cola over the course of a day, switch to something without caffeine for the last drinks of the day. Drink ginger ale, seltzer, or water at dinner and afterwards for two weeks. Then stop drinking caffeinated beverages after lunch. Within a few weeks, you will have cut back on the amount of caffeinated cola by more than half.

If coffee is your drink of choice, you can cut back on caffeine gradually in several ways. Either slowly cut back on the amount of coffee you drink or slowly replace caffeinated coffee with decaffeinated. If you stop off and buy a sixteen-ounce cup of coffee at a convenience store every morning, start reaching for a smaller cup. Switch to drinking decaffeinated coffee instead of caffeinated coffee after dinner.

Another technique would be to switch from drinking coffee to drinking the same amount of tea. Tea has less caffeine per ounce than coffee, so switching will reduce caffeine intake.

Or you can reduce your caffeine intake by mixing decaffeinated and caffeinated coffee. When you make your coffee, use two-thirds regular ground coffee to one-third decaffeinated ground coffee the first week. The next week, use a mixture of half caffeinated and half decaffeinated. By the third or fourth week, you can be using 100 percent decaffeinated.

You can do this elsewhere, also. Some convenience stores allow you to pour your own coffee. Fill your cup half with caffeinated coffee and half with decaffeinated coffee. Many coffee shops also offer "half-caf" coffee, espresso, and cappuccino.

It is true that decaffeinated coffee may not have all the flavor of regular coffee. If the idea of drinking decaffeinated coffee does not appeal to you, try using whole-bean decaffeinated coffee that you grind right before you make the coffee. Ground coffee loses flavor as it sits, so using freshly ground decaffeinated coffee may make a difference. Making really good decaffeinated coffee is worth the effort. You might also try using a flavored decaffeinated coffee—such as hazelnut, cinnamon, or vanilla—or switching to a darker roast of coffee. The proper way to make a good cup of coffee—caffeinated or decaffeinated—is described in the Appendix.

You might also try drinking hot chocolate, which has far less caffeine than coffee (even when the theobromine content is considered, hot chocolate is less stimulating than coffee), or drinking herbal teas such as chamomile, peppermint, or

Tea has less caffeine per ounce than coffee. Switching to tea would reduce caffeine intake. Here, workers carry freshly picked tea leaves to weighing stations. Much of the work in the tea harvest is done by women.

caffeine-free mixtures. You can also try drinking hot apple cider or having a cup of broth. Recipes for some caffeine-free hot drinks are in the Appendix.

Decaffeinated coffee is easy to find. It is sold as beans, as ground coffee, and as instant coffee. Coffee shops and restaurants that serve coffee almost always serve decaffeinated coffee as well. Gourmet coffee shops and coffeehouses will usually sell decaffeinated espresso and cappuccino as well.

Similarly, decaffeinated tea is available both as loose tea and in tea bags. Decaffeinated bottled iced tea and iced tea mix are also sold in supermarkets. Another choice would be herbal tea mixtures such as chamomile or peppermint tea, which do not contain caffeine.

Caffeine-free colas are available at supermarkets. The two major manufacturers of colas sell caffeine-free versions of their colas. However, decaffeinated cola may be easier to find on supermarket shelves than in a soft-drink machine. If a caffeine-free cola is not available, other soft drinks such as ginger ale, most root beers, and many fruit-flavored beverages do not contain caffeine and can be used as an alternative.

An alternative to eating chocolate is carob, a natural product that has a taste very similar to chocolate but does not contain caffeine. Carob is available in health food stores in the form of candy bars and drink mixes.

If you are reducing the amount of caffeine you take in, start to read product labels, especially the list of ingredients. Most clear non-cola sodas do not contain caffeine but some do. Some fruit-flavored energy drinks contain caffeine. The best way to ensure you are not drinking a beverage with caffeine is to look for the words "caffeine-free" on the label.

The Amount of Caffeine in Chocolate
(in milligrams)

Type of Chocolate	Average per Ounce	Range per Ounce
COCOA BEVERAGE (5 OUNCES)	4	2–20
CHOCOLATE MILK (8 OUNCES)	5	2–7
MILK CHOCOLATE (I OUNCE)	6	1–15
DARK SEMISWEET CHOCOLATE (I OUNCE)	20	5–35
BAKING CHOCOLATE (UNSWEETENED) (I OUNCE)	26	26
CHOCOLATE SYRUP (I OUNCE)	4	4

Source: U.S. Food and Drug Administration, Food Additive Chemistry Evaluation Branch.

If you try to quit drinking caffeine and fail, don't be disheartened. Changing any long-standing pattern in your life is not easy. If you find yourself slipping back into your old caffeine habits, try again to quit or cut back. You may need to try several times because breaking a habit is hard. Even if you only cut back on the amount of caffeine you use, you will have done well.

Questions for Discussion

1. At what age do you think it is acceptable to start using caffeine?

2. If you consume caffeine, did you start consuming it because of the way your family uses it?

3. Do you think that children under the age of twelve should drink coffee? What about iced tea or cola?

5

Personal Aspects of Caffeine

Most people learn to consume caffeine at home with their families. In some cultures, children are allowed to drink coffee at an early age. In others, children are not introduced to coffee until they are teenagers or adults. Within cultures, caffeine use may also vary from family to family. Families that may not allow their children to have coffee may allow them to have caffeinated cola beverages or tea.

Some cultures that have strict prohibitions against the use of alcohol have no problem with the use of caffeine. Coffee drinking is a common practice in many Islamic cultures, where alcohol is forbidden. In Turkey, for example, very strong coffee is brewed and enjoyed with family and friends. In other cultures, caffeine is considered a drug and is not allowed.

Families that do not allow their children to have coffee may allow them
to take in other sources of caffeine such as tea or chocolate. Here,
cocoa powder, made from cocoa beans, is pressed into cakes as one
part of the processing of cocoa into chocolate.

Mormons

The use of coffee and tea are prohibited by the teachings of the Church of Jesus Christ of Latter-day Saints, the Mormons, which was organized in 1830. Joseph Smith, the church's founder, is said to have received a revelation from God about health practices. This revelation prohibits the use of both alcoholic beverages and hot beverages, which Mormons interpret to mean coffee and tea.[1]

Although caffeine is not specifically mentioned by name, Mormons are also prohibited from using "substances that are harmful to the body," which most Mormons interpret to include caffeine. Therefore, in addition to abstaining from coffee and tea, most Mormons do not drink colas or other soft drinks with caffeine. Because of the prohibition against coffee and tea, decaffeinated coffee and tea and iced tea and coffee are prohibited as well.

Many Mormons drink a hot coffee substitute made from roasted grain or roasted chicory roots. They also enjoy hot herbal teas such as chamomile tea.

Christian Scientists

Member of The Church of Christ, Scientist, also known as the Christian Scientists, also avoid coffee and caffeine for the most part, but the decision as to whether to use coffee, tea, or caffeine is left to the individual.

The church was founded by Mary Baker Eddy in the late 1800s and much of the teachings of the church are based on her book, *Science and Health with Key to the Scriptures*. In that book, she wrote that people should not have a "depraved appetite" for

tea and coffee since they destroy the "mind's control of the body."[2] Christian Scientists believe that they must rely on God's power and not on such things as drugs.

Many Christian Scientists do drink coffee and tea since such decisions are left to each individual. However, those who do use caffeine take care not to become dependent on it or to use caffeine to avoid fatigue or do more work.

Seventh Day Adventists

Like Mormons and Christian Scientists, Seventh Day Adventists also try to avoid coffee, tea, and other sources of caffeine. Seventh Day Adventists also abstain from alcohol and tobacco, and discourage the eating of meat, especially pork.

The church officially discourages the use of caffeine for health reasons and because it can change the body's functioning. Decaffeinated coffee, tea, and cola are enjoyed, however.

Caffeine Use in the Family

Most people who use caffeine first come in contact with it in their home. In some homes, a pot of coffee is always present on the stove during the day, while in others coffee is only made and consumed in the morning. Similarly, for some families cola accompanies every meal and is the common drink of choice, while in other families cola is rarely served in the home.

Patterns of caffeine use may change during the year. Summer may bring an increase in caffeine use because the family drinks iced tea in addition to the morning coffee. In winter, hot cocoa may be a common winter drink or snack.

In general, children pick up their family's attitude toward caffeine. However, children usually do not drink coffee since it is

Caffeine intake varies from person to person and beverage to beverage. Espresso has about as much caffeine per serving as regular coffee, but the serving sizes differ greatly. The small cup on the left is an espresso cup and holds a two-ounce serving. The cup on the right is a large coffee mug, and can hold a ten-ounce serving of medium-strength brewed coffee. The two servings would both provide between 200 and 250 milligrams of caffeine.

bitter tasting unless milk and sugar are added. A taste for coffee is usually acquired during the teen years or as a young adult. Cola, because it is sweetened and flavored, is widely consumed by children, as is iced tea.

Families should be aware of their patterns of caffeine consumption and keep in mind that each family member's habits may be mimicked by other family members, especially children. If the children in the family appear to be getting too much caffeine, it may be wise to cut back. Decaffeinated iced tea or caffeine-free colas or other soft drinks can be enjoyed safely by everyone and make a good choice for younger children.

Questions for Discussion

1. Do you think your family's caffeine use has affected how you view caffeine?

2. Do you know anyone who does not consume caffeine because of religious or cultural reasons?

3. If you consume caffeine, at what age did you start? Was that before or after other people your age?

6

Learning Moderation with Caffeine

In American society, caffeine is extremely easy to get. Because coffee, tea, and cola are so readily available, many people can become dependent on caffeine. Worse, they may not even realize where their jitters and nervousness or other side effects are coming from. If they do identify their symptoms with caffeine, they may cut out the one cup of coffee they consume occasionally but not cut back on the several cans of cola or bottles of iced tea they consume daily.

Caffeine dependence can have a very gradual onset and most people do not notice the effects until they are older. As they age, many people start waking up in the middle of the night or have trouble getting to sleep. They may decide to skip the after-dinner coffee or avoid any caffeine after mid-afternoon to help this problem. However, teenagers can be affected by caffeine overdoses just as badly as adults can.

Most children do not drink coffee, the most concentrated source of caffeine. Many parents may allow their children to drink only hot cocoa, which is low in caffeine, or caffeine-free colas. For the most part, people start to drink larger amounts of caffeine as they enter their teens and early twenties, although this pattern can vary with different cultural groups.

For teenagers and college students, caffeine can become a study aid, enabling them to wake up for an early-morning class and keeping them alert for late-night studying. In addition to learning to drink coffee, some college students start to enjoy espresso at college coffeehouses. College students or young adults who must work night hours may also start to depend on caffeine tablets that are available over the counter.

Tablets of caffeine usually contain between 100 and 200 milligrams of caffeine. A seven-ounce cup of coffee usually contains between 80 and 175 milligrams of caffeine, so one caffeine tablet, depending on the brand, has the same amount of caffeine as in one or two cups of coffee. A 200-milligram tablet of caffeine may not be too much by itself, but some people take caffeine tablets in addition to drinking coffee and cola.

A large dose of caffeine taken over too short a period of time—say a cola earlier in the day plus a large mug of coffee plus a caffeine tablet—may help prevent sleepiness but it will bring on caffeine jitters and nervousness. Because caffeine takes several hours to be eliminated from the body, if you take a large amount of caffeine you will probably stay awake longer than you need to. You may be unable to sleep when you finally go to bed.

The Amount of Caffeine in Medication
(in milligrams)

Prescription Medication	Amount
CAFERGOT™(FOR MIGRAINE HEADACHES)	100
FIORINOL™ (FOR TENSION HEADACHES)	40
SOMA™ (FOR PAIN RELIEF, MUSCLE RELAXANT)	32
DARVON COMPOUND™ (FOR PAIN RELIEF)	32.4

Non-Prescription Medication	Amount
VIVARIN™(FOR ALERTNESS)	200
NO-DOZ™(FOR ALERTNESS)	100
EXCEDRIN™ (FOR PAIN RELIEF)	65
ANACIN™(FOR PAIN RELIEF)	32
MIDOL™(FOR PAIN RELIEF)	32.4

Source: FDA National Center for Drugs Biologics
*This list contains only a sampling of medications that contain caffeine.
It is by no means meant to be an exhaustive listing of every medication
on the market that contains caffeine.*

The key to reducing dependence on caffeine is avoiding it or reducing the amount you take in. Some people may be so sensitive to caffeine that they must eliminate it entirely from their diet. Others must avoid caffeine for health reasons such as hypoglycemia. However, most people do not have a problem with caffeine when they use it in moderation.

What is moderation? A moderate amount of caffeine varies from person to person. The amount that gives no side effects to one person could leave the next person with shaking hands and a headache. If you have no caffeine side effects, you may not need to cut back. However, just because side effects may not be visible to you does not mean they do not exist. If you experience jitters, sleep problems, stomach problems, or anxiety, you may be taking in too much caffeine.

Caffeine is like alcohol in one sense: If you think you might have a problem with alcohol, you probably do. Similarly, if it crosses your mind that you might need to cut back on caffeine, you probably should.

One young person who decided to cut back on the amount of coffee he consumes is Samuel Mikes, a nineteen-year-old student at Harvey Mudd College in Claremont, California.[1] Sam started to enjoy coffee when he was fifteen years old.

Sam's parents both consume coffee at breakfast and dinner and occasionally consume iced coffee, he said. As a child, he did not like the taste of coffee.

"I started to drink coffee on a trip to Europe," Sam said. In Europe, coffee is usually made stronger than it is in the United States, using more coffee grounds per cup and darker roast beans. His coffee habit solidified when he was an exchange student staying with a family in Finland.

"In that family, it was coffee before breakfast and then coffee with breakfast and with lunch and with dinner," he said.

In high school and during his first year of college, Sam usually filled a twenty-four-ounce insulated container with strong black coffee in the morning, so he would have it during the day. Because he enjoys good coffee, he bought gourmet blends of coffee and ground it himself. He started to become dependent on the coffee to wake up. "I didn't want to go to classes in the morning without my morning coffee," he said.

Sam started to notice that his fingers shook a little, not enough to interfere with writing or typing, but a noticeable amount. He also started to feel a bit jittery and was getting mild stomach upsets. The upset stomachs were more severe if he had more coffee than usual. His sleep patterns were also becoming slightly disturbed.

"As it is, I'm on an abbreviated sleep schedule," he said. "I didn't want any more interference."

Sam now limits himself to a can of cola in the morning. If he doesn't have cola in the morning, he may have a cup of coffee in the afternoon. He never has both, he said. He does not drink tea or eat chocolate, so the cola or the coffee are his only sources of caffeine.

Because he decided to cut back on his amount of caffeine abruptly, Sam did suffer some mild symptoms of withdrawal, although he thinks the word withdrawal may be too strong. "I was watching for it but I wouldn't say I went through anything that resembled withdrawal," he said. Still, he had a mild headache for a few days and was a bit irritable, he said.

Sam went from about 300 to 400 milligrams of caffeine a day to between 35 and 100 milligrams daily. An abrupt change

Sam limited his caffeine to either one can of cola or one cup of coffee a day. Shown here are cocoa plants and their pods. Each pod contains thirty to forty cocoa beans.

like that can bring on withdrawal symptoms in most people. Sam chose to cut back abruptly rather than reducing his intake gradually. The abrupt change worked for him. However, he knew he could try to cut back gradually if he failed the first time.

He also chose not to try decaffeinated coffee. "I like the taste of coffee and the feeling of caffeine," Sam said. As a coffee lover, he pointed out that he cut back on caffeine because he decided he was getting too much. He has friends who consume more coffee than he ever did and who have no side effects. The side effects that he did have, although they were enough to make him decide to cut back, were not severe. "I've never had a bad experience with caffeine, in my opinion," he said.

Joan Vos MacDonald also had a problem with caffeine.[2]

"When I was in my late teens, I liked staying up all night and I drank a lot of coffee," she said. Her coffee habit reached a level of about ten mugfuls per day, she said.

"I used to go out to dance clubs and dance all night," Joan said. When she was eighteen and nineteen, she was a model living on her own in New York City. She didn't eat a lot since she was usually trying to lose weight and also smoked. "It was a bad combination of eating badly, smoking, and drinking a lot of coffee," she said.

Joan was diagnosed as having hypoglycemia when she was nineteen. Hypoglycemia (also called low blood sugar) is a condition where the glucose levels in the blood are abnormally low. (Glucose is the sugar that the body uses as an energy source during metabolism.) Normally, blood sugar levels are relatively stable, but with hypoglycemia they may be unstable and go up and down unpredictably.

One symptom of hypoglycemia is mood swings. Caffeine can increase the instability of blood sugar levels because it speeds

Chocolate could be harmful to a person with hypoglycemia not only because of the sugar, but because of the caffeine. Here, chocolate is being mixed into chocolate formulations. Chocolate formulations include milk chocolate, and semi-sweet or dark chocolate.

up the metabolism a bit after it reaches the bloodstream, throwing off blood sugar levels.

"I would sort of live on coffee and when I ran out, my mood would crash," Joan said.

Joan started to limit her intake of coffee. She allowed herself only two or three cups of coffee a day and spaced them out over the course of the day. "That is the absolute maximum I can have," she said. "I'd probably drink as much now as I used to if it didn't make me feel sick or affect my moods."

"I would periodically try to quit drinking coffee completely. Even when I made it past the withdrawal headache, I couldn't. Coffee is everywhere and it smells so good I would give in and have a cup," she said. Finally, within the last year, Joan was able to stop drinking coffee completely.

Both Sam and Joan realized that they had a problem with caffeine and did something about it. Both of them were able to cut back on the amount of caffeine they used with relatively few problems. They still enjoy coffee and caffeine on a daily basis, but they keep careful track of how much they consume.

Caffeine is like many things in life. It is enjoyable and has beneficial qualities, but it can be harmful when taken to excess. You can use caffeine, but you should not let caffeine use you. You can also easily live without caffeine. You do not have to drink coffee, tea, or cola and if you do choose to have them, you can have decaffeinated versions.

If you enjoy caffeine and have no problems with the amount you consume, good. If you think you are having a problem with caffeine, either cut back on how much you consume or cut it out altogether.

Questions for Discussion

1. Do you feel that you or anyone you know has a problem with caffeine?

2. Do you and your family keep beverages on hand that do not contain caffeine for guests who do not consume caffeine?

3. Do you think you would have a problem socially if you gave up caffeine?

Appendix

If you choose to avoid coffee and tea entirely, there are other beverages you can enjoy that contain no caffeine. Soft-drink machines usually stock ginger ale, lemon soda, and other caffeine-free beverages. Most stores stock a large variety of bottled fruit juices, seltzers, and lemonades.

How to Make a Good Cup of Coffee

Coffee—with or without caffeine—is not hard to make. A well-prepared cup of decaffeinated coffee will taste better than a bad cup of coffee with caffeine.

First, start with good water. Since water is the largest ingredient in a cup of coffee, the taste of the water will affect the taste of the coffee. If your tap water tastes of chlorine, it might be better to make coffee using filtered water or bottled spring water.

Next, buy good coffee. The best coffee is made of whole beans that are ground right before your make the coffee. Freshly ground coffee tastes better. If you buy coffee already ground, keep the ground coffee in a sealed container in the refrigerator and do not buy so much at one time that it grows stale before you use it. You could also store ground coffee in a sealed container in the freezer.

91

There are two common methods of making coffee, the drip method and the percolator method. Most automatic coffee makers use the drip method, where water near boiling temperature is dripped through ground coffee into a carafe. Drip method coffee can also be made using a filter holder that fits either on top of a carafe or on top of a mug. Because drip coffee is filtered, it usually has little sediment and a cleaner taste.

In a percolator, boiling water is circulated continuously for several minutes through a basket holding ground coffee. Percolated coffee is usually stronger than drip method coffee and it contains more oil from the coffee grounds, giving it a more bitter flavor. Percolated coffee can taste burned if the pot is left untended for too long, and a carafe of drip method coffee can also taste burned if it sits too long on the heater.

Most recipes for coffee call for using one or two tablespoons of ground coffee for each cup of water. This is a matter of individual taste and can be varied.

For drip method coffee, grind the coffee fine but not to a powder. Put a filter in the filter holder and place the filter holder over a carafe or cup. Measure out about one and a half tablespoons of coffee and put it in the filter. Press the coffee down gently. Bring water to a boil and then turn off the heat. Pour a small amount of water into the filter to wet the grounds thoroughly. Wait a minute and then pour more hot water through the grounds and let it drip into the carafe or cup.

Serve the coffee immediately. If a pot of coffee must sit before being served, it keeps better in an insulated container than on a hot plate or stove. Coffee that has been sitting on a heating element for more than an hour or so will always taste burned. A good insulated container will usually keep coffee hot for several hours without any burned taste.

Making a Good Cup of Tea

As with coffee, the quality of the water is important to the quality of a cup of tea. Fresh tea also makes a better cup than stale tea that has been on the shelf for too long.

The most convenient way to make tea is to use a tea bag. The process is so simple as to be almost impossible to foul up. Place the bag in the cup and pour boiling water in. Let the tea steep for two to  three minutes and remove the bag. Some herbal teas, notably chamomile, may need to be steeped longer for fuller flavor.

If you are using loose tea—and many herbal tea mixes do not come in tea bags—you can either use a tea ball or a teapot and strainer. A tea ball is a small perforated metal ball that can hold about a spoonful of tea leaves or herbs. The tea ball then is used just like a tea bag.

Using a ceramic or china teapot is simple. First, place heated water in the teapot for a few minutes to warm the pot and then empty the water out. Now spoon loose tea into the pot. The amount of tea you use varies with the type of herb and with your own preference. Pour boiling water into the pot and let the tea steep for two to three minutes. When you pour out the tea, pour it into the cup through a strainer to catch loose tea leaves.

Other Choices

If you choose to avoid coffee and tea entirely, there are other hot drinks you can enjoy.

Hot apple toddy—In a saucepan, heat up apple juice or apple cider. Place a cinnamon stick in a mug and pour in the hot juice. You can also add a dash of lemon juice.

Hot lemon toddy—In a saucepan, boil water. Place one or two teaspoons of sugar in a cup. Add one or two tablespoons of lemon juice and one cinnamon stick to the cup. Pour in the hot water and stir with the cinnamon stick. A variation on this drink is to use a few fresh or dried mint leaves instead of the cinnamon stick.

Swedish milk—Add a tablespoon full of molasses or brown sugar and a dash of cinnamon to a cup of hot whole milk or low-fat milk.

Cranberry glog—Heat a mixture of cranberry juice cocktail and grape juice. Add a teaspoon of sugar and a dash of cinnamon or nutmeg, or a cinnamon stick could be placed in each cup.

Hot broth—Use either canned or homemade beef or chicken broth or bouillon. (Low-salt broths are available or bouillon cubes can be used.) Heat the broth in either a saucepan on the stove or in a microwave-safe container in the microwave oven. A dash of hot pepper sauce or some curry powder can be added for flavor.

Chapter Notes

Chapter 1

1. "Coffee and Health," *Consumer Reports*, October, 1994, p. 650.

2. Ibid.

3. Chris W. Lecos, *Caffeine Jitters: Some Safety Questions Remain*, FDA Consumer, Vol. 21., No. 10, December 1987–January 1988, p. 26; "Caffeine Doesn't Mean Just Coffee Anymore," *FDA Consumer*, Vol. 21, No. 10, December 1987–January 1988, p. 26.

4. "Caffeine Doesn't Mean Just Coffee Anymore," p. 27.

5. Ibid.

6. *Consumer Reports*, p. 650.

7. Lecos, p. 25.

8. Ibid., p. 22.

9. Ibid.

10. Richard J. Gilbert, *Caffeine: The Most Popular Stimulant* (New York: Chelsea House Publishers, 1986), pp. 24–25.

11. Charles Panati, *Browser's Book of Beginnings: Origins of Everything Under (And Including) the Sun* (Boston: Houghton Mifflin Company, 1984), pp. 94–95.

12. "Coffee," *The World Book Encyclopedia*, Vol. C (Chicago: World Book, 1991), p. 755.

13. Ibid.

14. Ibid.

15. *Consumer Reports*, p. 650.

16. *The World Book Encyclopedia*, p. 754.

17. Gilbert, p. 28.

18. Michael Marriott and others, "Jiving with Java," *Newsweek*, February 13, 1995, p. 83.

19. Panati, pp. 92–94.

20. Gilbert, p. 27.

21. "Tea," *The World Book Encyclopedia*, Vol. T (Chicago: World Book, 1991), p. 63.

22. Ibid., pp. 63–64.

23. Ibid., p. 64.

24. Ibid., pp. 62–63.

25. "Chocolate," *The World Book Encyclopedia*, Vol. C (Chicago: World Book, 1991), p. 517.

26. Panati, pp. 121–122.

27. Marcia Morton and Frederick Morton, *Chocolate: An Illustrated History* (New York: Crown Publishers, 1986), p. 3.

28. *The World Book Encyclopedia*, pp. 517–518.

29. Morton and Morton, p. 4.

30. Ibid., pp. 9–11.

31. *The World Book Encyclopedia*, pp. 518–519.

32. "Kola Nut," *The World Book Encyclopedia*, Vol. K (Chicago: World Book, 1991), p. 363.

33. Panati, p. 97.

34. Gilbert, pp. 33–35.

35. Ibid.

36. Ibid., p. 42.

37. Ibid., p. 33.

Chapter 2

1. "Caffeine," *The World Book Encyclopedia*, Vol. C (Chicago: World Book, 1991), p. 14; *Tea and Caffeine* (New York: The Tea Council of the USA) (undated, not paged).

2. "Caffeine and Health: Clarifying the Controversies," *IFIC Review*, May 1993, pp. 1–7.

3 Richard J. Gilbert, *Caffeine: The Most Popular Stimulant*, (New York: Chelsea House Publishers, 1991), p. 28.

4. Ibid., p. 49.

5. Ibid., pp. 42–43.

6. Ibid., pp. 44–45.

7. Neal L. Benowitz, "Clinical Pharmacology of Caffeine," *Annual Review of Medicine*, Vol. 41, 1990, pp. 277–288.

8. "Coffee and Health," *Consumer Reports*, October 1994, p. 650.

9. *Tea and Caffeine*, (not paged).

10. Ibid.

11. *Consumer Reports*, p. 650.

12. *Tea and Caffeine; Coffee Update*.

13. Ibid.; Chris W. Lecos, "Caffeine Jitters: Some Safety Questions Remain," *FDA Consumer*, Vol. 21, No. 10, December 1987–January 1988, p. 23.

14. *Consumer Reports*, pp. 650–651.

15. *Tea and Caffeine; Coffee Update*, (not paged).

16. *Consumer Reports*, p. 650.

17. Ibid.

18. Lecos, p. 23.

19. Ibid.; *IFIC Review*, p. 25.

20. Ibid.

21. Ibid., p. 20.

22. Ibid., p. 24.

23. *Consumer Reports*, p. 651.

24. Gilbert, p. 79.

25. *Consumer Reports*, p. 651.

26. *IFIC Review*, pp. 1–7.

27. Lecos, p. 24.

28. *IFIC Review*, pp. 1–7.

29. Ibid.

30. Gilbert, p. 42; Marcia Morton and Frederick Morton, *Chocolate: An Illustrated History*, (New York: Crown Publishers, 1986), p. 148.

31. Gilbert, p. 42.

32. Morton and Morton, p. 148.

33. Gilbert, pp. 106–107.

34. *Tea and Caffeine*, (not paged).

35. Gilbert, p. 108.

36. Ibid., pp. 108–109.

37. *Consumer Reports*, p. 650.

Chapter 3

1 "Drug Abuse," *The World Book Encyclopedia*, Vol. D (Chicago: World Book, 1991), p. 364.

2. Neal L. Benowitz, "Clinical Pharmacology of Caffeine," *Annual Review of Medicine*, Vol. 41, 1990, pp. 277–288.

3. Eric C. Strain, Geoffrey K. Mumford, Kenneth Silverman, and Roland Griffiths, "Caffeine Dependence Syndrome: Evidence from Case Histories and Experimental Evaluations." *JAMA: The Journal of the American Medical Association,* Vol. 272, No. 13, October 5, 1994, pp. 1043–1048.

4. Ibid., p. 1047

5. Ibid.

6. Benowitz, pp. 277–288.

7. Richard M. Glass, "Caffeine Dependence: What Are the Implications?" *JAMA: The Journal of the American Medical Association.* Vol. 272, No. 13, October 5, 1994, p. 1066.

8. Ibid.

Chapter 4

1. Richard M. Glass, "Caffeine Dependence: What Are the Implications?" *JAMA: The Journal of the American Medical Association.* Vol. 272, No. 13, October 5, 1994, p. 1065.

2. Ibid.

3. Richard J. Gilbert, *Caffeine: The Most Popular Stimulant* (New York: Chelsea House Publishers, 1986), pp. 134–135.

4. Ibid.

5. Glass, p. 1066.

Chapter 5

1. The Church of Jesus Christ of Latter-day Saints, *Press Book,* (Salt Lake City, Utah), July 1991.

2. Mary Baker Eddy, *Science and Health with Keys to the Scriptures,* (Boston: Christian Science Publishing Society, 1994), pp. 80, 406.

Chapter 6

1. Personal interview with Samuel Mikes, February and March, 1995.

2. Personal interview with Joan Vos MacDonald, March, April, and December, 1995.

Glossary

addiction—Physical or psychological dependence on a drug.

adenosine—A chemical in the body that helps regulate body processes, notably the transmission of signals by nerves.

analgesic—Any medication that relieves pain.

anxiety—A feeling of worry, uneasiness, dread, or apprehension.

caffeine—A methylxanthine drug that stimulates the central nervous system. Found in coffee beans, tea, kola nuts, cocoa, maté leaves, guarana seeds, and many other plants.

cappuccino—A beverage made with coffee, steamed milk, and milk foam or whipped cream. Usually served sweetened with a dusting of cinnamon or cocoa on top.

cardiovascular system—The heart and blood vessels, responsible for circulating blood through the body.

central nervous system—The brain and spinal cord, responsible for mental function and higher nerve function.

decaffeination—The process of removing caffeine from any product that contains it naturally, such as coffee or tea.

dependence—A physical or psychological craving for a drug.

espresso—A type of strong coffee frequently served black.

gastrointestinal system—The esophagus, stomach, and intestines, responsible for digestion of food and elimination of waste products.

half-life—The length of time it takes the body to eliminate half of a dose of a drug or substance.

insomnia—Inability to sleep or interrupted sleep.

metabolism—The process of breaking down substances within the body. The body metabolizes substances in food into either energy or material it can use in repair and other activities.

methylxanthine—Any of a class of drugs that includes caffeine, theobromine, and theophylline.

psychoactive drug—Any drug that has an effect on the mental state or which is able to affect mood and behavior.

stimulant—Any drug that can increase body function or activity.

theobromine—A methylxanthine drug that is a stimulant, found in cocoa, tea, and kola nuts. Acts similarly to caffeine but is less potent.

theophylline—A methylxanthine drug that is a stimulant for the heart and breathing. Used medically to treat lung conditions such as asthma, emphysema, and bronchitis.

tolerance—The process in which someone becomes accustomed to using a drug so that the drug no longer has an effect. An increased amount of the drug is then needed to produce an effect comparable to that formerly provided by the lower amount.

withdrawal—The process of ridding the body of a chemical on which it has become dependent.

Further Reading

Gilbert, Richard M. *Caffeine: The Most Popular Stimulant*. New York: Chelsea House Publishers, 1986.

Goulart, Frances Sheridan. *The Caffeine Book*. New York: Dodd, Mead & Co., 1984.

Lecos, Chris W. "Caffeine Jitters: Some Safety Questions Remain," *FDA Consumer*, December, 1987.

Morton, Marcia, and Morton, Frederick. *Chocolate: An Illustrated History*. New York: Crown Publishers, 1986.

Panati, Charles. *Browser's Book of Beginnings*. Boston: Houghton Mifflin Co., 1984.

Index

103

China
tea and, 14
chocolate
caffeine in, 18
history of, 17–18
manufacturing of, 18
Christian Scientists, 75–76
cocoa beans, 17–18 (*See also:* chocolate)
coffee
amount of caffeine in, 12, 38, 40, 42
history of, 10
how to make, 91–92
popularity of, 6
regular use of, 6,
serving size of, 38
social use of, 12
species, 9
where grown, 9–10, 12
coffeehouses, 10, 13, 44
cola
amount of caffeine in, 20, 42–43
cup size, 38
history of, 19, 21
popularity of, 6
species, 19

D
decaffeinated coffee and tea, 38, 67, 69
amount of caffeine left in, 22, 40
decaffeination, 21–22
drug dependence, 51, 80

E
espresso, 13, 38

G
Glass, Dr. Richard, 60
guarana, 25

H
herbal tea, 15, 67
hypoglycemia, 36, 65, 86

I
iced tea, 15, 38, 62

instant coffee, 12
instant tea, 15

K
kola nuts, 19

M
MacDonald, Joan Vos, 86, 88
maté, 25
Mayas, 17
medications, 22, 43
methylxanthine, 25, 26
Mikes, Samuel, 83–84, 86
moderation, 80–81, 83–84, 86, 88
Mormons, 75

P
pain relievers, 43

S
Seventh Day Adventists, 76
soft drinks, 19–21
stimulants, 25, 28

T
tea
amount of caffeine in, 40, 42
first use of, 14
history of, 14–15
how to make, 93
types of, 15
theine, 26
Theobroma cacao (cocoa plant), 17
theobromine, 18, 26, 28, 43
theophylline, 18, 22, 26, 28, 31, 43
tobacco
and caffeine metabolism, 28
Toltecs, 17

W
withdrawal, 58, 66

Y
yerba maté, 25